IMAGES
of Wales

AROUND
RHONDDA FAWR

'FROM A BOY TO A MAN'

Part One – The Day of Signing

'Lad it's time to wear long trousers,
You're old enough to sign on in the pit,
Time to bring a wage home, help your Mam.
Earn your keep: after all, son, you're now thirteen.
I know, lad, you're a bit scrawny, no muscle,
But you're fit, unlike others, you're well.
Let's see Evans the cobbler, get workboots,
Second-hand, solid ones, ideal for the pit.
Now don't listen to the gossips, it's not as bad as hell;
Even so, it's black and cramped down there, lad.
You'll get along fine son, I can tell.

Part Two – First Pay Day

The eldest of seven, with the looks of his Dad,
Wends his weary way home, through cobblestone streets.
Muscles aching beyond compare, face blackened
With dust and grit; eyes white in contrast, casting
An eerie sort of glare. Pride wells in his chest:
He carries his first pay home, to give to his Mam,
In exchange for a hot tub of water, to bathe away
The day's dirt, in front of a welcoming coal fire.
Thoughts fill the lad's mind, he feels different now;
A week of work, drawing pay, somehow he grew,
Prematurely, from being a boy into a man today.

Part Three – Disaster

Fear fills hearts, as the hooter calls out of time,
Echoing through the valley, a warning for all. Disaster!
An explosion had sounded, deep below. How many dead?
It was too soon, impossible to know. The lad for certain,
He would face grief, he'd done his shift; Dad was his relief.
Women gathered, sobbing from worry and strain,
The watching lad crumbles, feeling like a boy again.
Hours pass, the rescue party bring up pitiful remains.
Lad's Mam wails, it was Dad's last shift, his last journey home,
To be laid in the front room, where Mam mourns alone.
Other women scream, in all fifty-three miners are dead.
They curse the black gold, and the managers of the pit head.

Part Four – Sad Goodbyes

Grief fills the valley, in pain the people gather,
As slowly the sombre miners break out in song,
Singing sad laments for their colleagues who've gone.
The lad heads the funeral cortège on this sad day:
Tears he sees on the women, as men to God pray.
It's now in this moment, this lad is truly born the man,
Now having to earn as much money for his Mam.
Six hungry young mouths he works to feed,
The man of the house, aware of their poverty and need.
Fear fills his heart, wondering if it could happen to be
That he himself may die, one day, in a mining tragedy.

by Elaine Hawkins

IMAGES
of Wales

AROUND
RHONDDA FAWR

Compiled by
Avril Evans and Elaine Hawkins

TEMPUS

First published 1999
Copyright © Avril Evans and Elaine Hawkins, 1999

Tempus Publishing Limited
The Mill, Brimscombe Port,
Stroud, Gloucestershire, GL5 2QG

ISBN 0 7524 1590 5

Typesetting and origination by
Tempus Publishing Limited
Printed in Great Britain by
Midway Clark Printing, Wiltshire

Contents

The co-authors of this book are: (left) Elaine Hawkins, here seen in 1966 aged two and a half years, and (below) Avril Evans, seen here at the age of two in 1960.

Foreword

Walking each day along the streets that wend their way through this valley creates the thought that we ourselves are walking the same paths that our ancestors have laid. Year after year as we grow older, it suddenly dawns on us that we, in the course of our own lives, have become a part of the very same history that tells the story of the valleys. After all, have we not ourselves helped to reshape the face of an ever changing valley, that refuses to be left behind the rest of the world and its naturally constant progression? In these thoughts, it is hard to imagine that one day our own children and grandchildren will undoubtedly walk the very same valley streets and wonder themselves what contribution we made in forming the face of the valley as they will know it.

We have hope in our hearts that the generations who follow in our footsteps will carry within themselves the same pride and love for their inheritance of the valley as we ourselves do.

Elaine Hawkins and Avril Evans

Introduction

I have lived all my life in the Rhondda. I have seen many changes, for good and bad. I remember using pen and ink in primary school, ink monitors and pink blotting paper. I still remember the scratch of the old detachable nibs on paper and ceramic inkpots in rows of old wooden desks, that were themselves covered in ink and marked with the graffiti of decades of schoolchildren's hands. It meant very little to me then and I hardly foresaw that, in a short span of years, biros would replace the old ink pens and computers would be commonplace in school.

The changes, though gradual when lived through, can be seen as momentous in hindsight, but it is all too easy to look back at the past and see it through rose-tinted spectacles. Nostalgia takes the place of reality and we lose sight of the hardship that was a common bedfellow of most people back then. In these terms things have certainly improved – people have more money, better living conditions, better mobility and more opportunities. However, we may have destroyed many enemies of the past, such as poor housing, disease, poverty and starvation, but there is also the danger that we are destroying our friends too.

Modernization can bring elitism, the loss of community, a loss of pride in what we have achieved, the loss of hope, leading to alienation and loneliness. The past conditions may have been hard but the community spirit was strong and it was this that put down the firm foundations and created a strong, forward-looking, determined people. For today's youth, the Rhondda can seem stagnant and immobile with a lack of opportunity. There is a strong case for this argument and there is nothing wrong with wanting to grow and better oneself, to reach out to the wider world outside the Rhondda. But there is also something to be gained by remembering our roots, remembering the firm foundations our grandparents put down, for it was these people, who with their grit and determination, their refusal to give in to what at times must have been a hard existence, that made us today, the valley people: a proud and determined race.

Avril Evans

'A JEWEL IN GOD'S WORLDLY CROWN'

Amidst the company of forestry trees,
Shaded by woodland, I lie in rich green fern,
Listening to the songs of the wind.
Distant baaing of grazing sheep is carried,
As soothing melodies, on the soft summer breeze.
I watch the sun spray flecks of spun gold down;
Shimmering, they dance as spectral visions,
Upon rustling leaves, so full of graceful intent.
I savour the scents of fallen bark and moss,
Pine needles and withered brown leaves;
The odours mingle to linger, fragrancing the air,
High on the mountain, covered in lush greens.
I turn my eye to view the valley below:
Peace overwhelms me, easing me quietly
Into oblivious serenity, causing pangs of emotion,
That create longings and deep wishes,
Feeling my wish, wanting to stay here,
Encapsulated in this moment, this place, forever.
So grateful am I, the slag heaps have gone,
Replaced by this beauty, of which the charm
I happily succumb to, loitering peacefully.
This place that I envision to be set, so perfectly,
As a jewel in God's worldly crown,
Until burns orange the setting sun
Around me, its rays of life reaching out,
Covering all in a chiffon-like haze. I stay,
Watching this blissful moment fade to its end,
Before making my way back to my home,
Deep in the heart of the Rhondda Valley.

by Elaine Hawkins

One
The War Years

An early tank, travelling through Pentre to commemorate the end of the First World War in 1918.

'8TH JANUARY 1917 – LAST THOUGHTS'

From eyes fades light, life becomes still,
Silence fills ears with calm, as all around,
Grotesque images fall to shadows in ditches.
From a battle not yet over, gunfire sounds,
As deafening thunder in an angry grey sky.
While here lies a fallen soldier, accepting his fate;
Skin pales, becoming as a waxen figure,
A mannequin, betraying his true self
In red stains, that trickle
From a corner of his parted lips.
His pain fades to darkness, peace descends:
For him, salvation from the hell he's seen today.
Far away in memories, as last moments slip away,
Forming in spectral visions, the mountains,
Below them the valley; he misses the place,
After all, it is his home.
Remembrances of a miner emerge,
Who later a soldier was made:
So far from the Rhondda Valley,
In this battle, the Battle of the Somme.
A wish fills his heart, such longing,
Why could he not have stayed?
Strange are the thoughts that fill his mind,
Suddenly – counting days, how many spent,
Digging in the darkness?
Forever it seemed, evading disasters,
Touching against the heart of death.
How many blue scars did he wear? Badges,
Standing as testament to his survival in the pit.
Lasting only to be here, to this his final day,
Suddenly it seemed so unfair, surviving
One kind of hell, one that caused
So many lungs to decay, to be faced
With this fate on another's soil.
But still dreams flutter, serenity finally descends,
Allowing last thoughts in eternal sleep
To fade away.

by Elaine Hawkins

William Thomas Jenkins (10.4.1874 –
3.1.1930). William left the Rhondda for health
reasons and went to British Columbia in the
belief that he would find work there.
Unfortunately, he found that only married men
with children were being allowed to sign on for
work. He decided then to travel to America,
but eventually settled in Australia. He married
a Scottish woman and had two daughters, Ivy
and Margaret. At home in the Rhondda,
William's family thought that they would never
see him again, but during the First World War
William joined the Army and was posted to
Andover. Despite the difficulties of mobility,
his sister Margaret and brother Arthur travelled
to Andover and asked at the camp gates for
'Willie Jenkins from Australia'. Amazingly he
was found, despite there being many other
Welsh boys at the camp. William was given
leave to come back to the Rhondda in order to
see his family for the last time. He gave his
sister Margaret a gold locket, which she
treasured. (Margaret is shown in the
photograph wearing the locket.) When the war
was over, William was sent back 'home' to
Australia, where he had signed on. When he
died, he was buried in Australia.

The late Cyril Harding of 'The Cottage', Maindy Road, Ton-Pentre, taken during his years in service.

Cyril Harding's service book for the period that he was in the army, during the Second World War.

'Lt. A.A' 2

(I) SOLDIER'S NAME and DESCRIPTION on ATTESTATION.

Army Number 6554319

Surname (in capitals) HARDING

Christian Names (in full) Cyril

Date of Birth 13/2/1917. Zellybehe -

Place of Birth. {
Parish ....
In or near the town of Treachy
In the county of Glam.
}

Trade on Enlistment Night Porter

Nationality of Father at birth British.

Nationality of Mother at birth British.

Religious Denomination C. of E.

Approved Society Prudential.

Membership No. 6007/218.

Enlisted at Yeovil. On 18/4/40

For the :—
* Regular Army.   * Supplementary Reserve.
* Territorial Army.   * Army Reserve Section D.
* Strike out those inapplicable.

For........years with the Colours and...........years in the Reserve.

Signature of Soldier Harding C.

Date April 22nd 1940

DESIGNATION.	Size
Greatcoats	5
Battle Dress Blouses	4
Battle Dress Trousers	4
Shorts	3
Pantaloons	.
Denim Overall Blouses	4
Cooks Jackets	.
Denim Overall Trousers	4
Cooks Trousers	.
Shirts	3
Woollen Vests	3
Woollen Drawers	3
Short Cell. Drawers	3
Jerseys Pullover	3
Jerkins Leather	3
Socks	2
Boots	7 5.
Hat	6 5/
	8

Date
Sign

Treharne Street, Cwmparc, on 9 October
1941 after a German air raid which
destroyed several houses.

VE Day celebrations, 8 May 1945. After six
years of warfare, it was difficult at first to
believe that victory had actually been
announced. However, despite the shortages
which still existed, valley people pooled
their rations and worked together making
cakes and decorations for the street parties
that were held from one end of the Rhondda
to the other.

Italian prisoners of war interned on the Isle of Man, 1941-42. In this picture are several men who later lived in the Rhondda Valley, including Mr Bracchi, the father of Mrs Dominica

Bacchetta (from the wool shop in Gelli) and Francesco Giovannone, Margo Giovannone's grandfather, from Ton-Pentre.

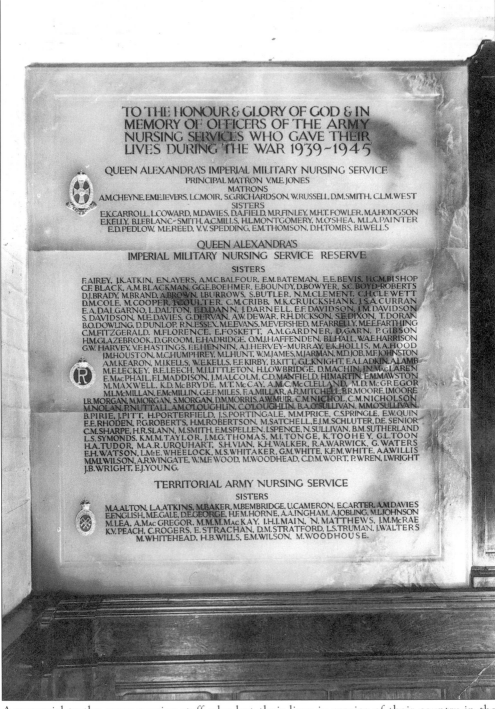

TO THE HONOUR & GLORY OF GOD & IN
MEMORY OF OFFICERS OF THE ARMY
NURSING SERVICES WHO GAVE THEIR
LIVES DURING THE WAR 1939~1945

QUEEN ALEXANDRA'S IMPERIAL MILITARY NURSING SERVICE
PRINCIPAL MATRON V.M.E.JONES
MATRONS
A.M.CHEYNE, E.M.E.IEVERS, L.C.MOIR, S.G.RICHARDSON, W.RUSSELL, D.M.SMITH, C.L.M.WEST
SISTERS
E.K.CARROLL, L.COWARD, M.DAVIES, D.A.FIELD, M.R.FINLEY, M.H.T.FOWLER, M.A.HODGSON
E.KELLY, B.LEBLANC-SMITH, A.C.MILLS, H.L.MONTGOMERY, M.O'SHEA, M.L.A.PAINTER
E.D.PEDLOW, M.E.REED, V.V.SPEDDING, E.M.THOMSON, D.H.TOMBS, B.I.WELLS

QUEEN ALEXANDRA'S
IMPERIAL MILITARY NURSING SERVICE RESERVE
SISTERS
F.AIREY, J.K.ATKIN, E.N.AYERS, A.M.C.BALFOUR, E.M.BATEMAN, E.E.BEVIS, H.C.M.BISHOP
C.F.BLACK, A.M.BLACKMAN, G.G.E.BOEHMER, E.BOUNDY, D.BOWYER, S.C.BOYD-ROBERTS
D.J.BRADY, M.BRAND, A.BROWN, I.BURROWS, S.BUTLER, N.M.CLEMENT, C.H.CLEWETT
D.M.COLE, M.COOPER, J.COULTER, C.M.CRIBB, M.K.CRUICKSHANK, J.S.A.CURRAN
E.A.DALGARNO, L.DALTON, E.D.DANN, J.DARNELL, E.F.DAVIDSON, J.M.DAVIDSON
S.DAVIDSON, M.E.DAVIES, G.DERVAN, A.W.DEWAR, R.H.DICKSON, S.E.DIXON, T.DORAN
B.O.DOWLING, D.DUNLOP, R.N.ESSEX, M.E.EVANS, M.EVERSHED, M.FARRELLY, M.E.FARTHING
C.M.FITZGERALD, M.FLORENCE, E.FOSKETT, A.M.GARDNER, D.GARN, P.GIBSON
H.M.GLAZEBROOK, D.GROOM, E.HADRIDGE, O.M.J.HAFFENDEN, B.I.HALL, W.A.E.HARRISON
G.W.HARVEY, V.E.HASTINGS, F.E.HENNIN, A.J.HERVEY-MURRAY, E.K.HOLLIS, M.A.HOOD
J.M.HOUSTON, M.C.HUMPHREY, M.I.HUNT, W.M.JAMES, M.JARMAN, M.D.JOB, M.F.JOHNSTON
A.M.KEARON, M.I.KELLS, W.E.KELLS, E.E.KIRBY, B.KITT, G.L.KNIGHT, E.A.LADKIN, A.LAMB
M.E.LECKEY, B.E.LEECH, M.J.LITTLETON, H.LOWBRIDGE, D.MACHIN, J.N.MacLAREN
E.MacPHAIL, F.L.MADDISON, J.MALCOLM, C.D.MANFIELD, H.I.MARTIN, E.M.MAWSTON
M.MAXWELL, K.D.McBRYDE, M.T.McCAY, A.M.C.McCLELLAND, M.D.McGREGOR
M.L.McMILLAN, E.McMILLIN, G.E.F.MILES, E.A.MILLAR, A.R.MITCHELL, B.R.MOORE, I.MOORE
I.B.MORGAN, M.MORGAN, S.MORGAN, D.M.MORRIS, A.W.MUIR, C.M.NICHOL, C.M.NICHOLSON
M.NOLAN, P.NUTTALL, A.M.O'LOUGHLIN, C.O'LOUGHLIN, B.A.O'SULLIVAN, M.M.O'SULLIVAN
B.PIRIE, J.PITT, H.PORTERFIELD, J.S.PORTINGALE, M.M.PRICE, C.S.PRINGLE, E.W.QUIN
E.E.RHODEN, P.G.ROBERTS, H.M.ROBERTSON, M.SATCHELL, E.J.M.SCHLUTER, D.E.SENIOR
C.M.SHARPE, H.R.SLANN, M.SMITH, E.M.SPELLEN, I.SPENCE, N.SULLIVAN, B.M.SUTHERLAND
L.S.SYMONDS, K.M.M.TAYLOR, J.M.G.THOMAS, M.I.TONGE, K.TOOHEY, G.L.TOON
H.A.TUDOR, M.A.R.URQUHART, S.H.VIAN, K.H.WALKER, R.A.WARWICK, G.WATERS
E.H.WATSON, L.M.E.WHEELOCK, M.S.WHITAKER, G.M.WHITE, K.F.M.WHITE, A.A.WILLIS
M.M.I.WILSON, A.R.WINGATE, W.M.F.WOOD, M.WOODHEAD, C.D.M.WORT, P.WREN, I.WRIGHT
J.B.WRIGHT, E.J.YOUNG.

TERRITORIAL ARMY NURSING SERVICE
SISTERS
M.A.ALTON, L.A.ATKINS, M.BAKER, M.BEMBRIDGE, U.CAMERON, E.CARTER, A.M.DAVIES
E.ENGLISH, M.E.GALE, D.E.GEORGE, H.F.M.HORNE, A.A.INGHAM, A.JOBLING, M.I.JOHNSON
M.LEA, A.MacGREGOR, M.M.M.MacKAY, I.H.I.MAIN, N.MATTHEWS, J.M.McRAE
K.V.PEACH, C.ROGERS, E.STRACHAN, D.M.STRATFORD, L.S.TRUMAN, J.WALTERS
M.WHITEHEAD, H.B.WILLS, E.M.WILSON, M.WOODHOUSE.

A memorial to the many nursing staff who lost their lives in service of their country in the
Second World War.

Margaret Eluned Davies of 88 Tyntyla Road, Llwynypia (second from the right), in East Africa in 1943. Margaret was a nursing sister with the Queen Alexandra's Imperial Military Nursing Service during the Second World War. She was just twenty-five years old when she was killed in action: on 12 February 1944, the ship on which she was serving, the SS *Khedive Ismail*, was torpedoed and sunk by a Japanese submarine in the area of the Maldives. The ship was carrying 1,324 troops and 183 crew including gunners; 137 crew members and 1,134 troops were lost. A harrowing account of the sinking of the ship has been related by a Mrs R.L.J. Wright, who was one of the few survivors of the tragedy. The ship had been part of a convoy which had sailed from Mombassa in February 1944 as a complete hospital, to join 11 East African Division in Ceylon. After being at sea for nearly a week, the ship was nearing the equator. On 12 February at 2 p.m., during a ship's concert on B deck, there was a terrific explosion, followed shortly thereafter by a second. In the time it took to stand up, the deck had listed sharply. Mrs Wright, being on the open deck, managed to jump into the sea and came up near a broken raft and was rescued. The convoy was disappearing over the horizon and all that was left of the *Khedive Ismail* were two upturned lifeboats, some broken and whole rafts, odd wreckage and one lifeboat right side up, in which there were very few people. The escorting Officer Cadet troops rowed around collecting any survivors, while two destroyers from the escort were dropping depth charges, which was terrifying for the survivors, being so close to the water. It was known that the enemy submarine was still hiding beneath them, but one ship had to risk stopping to pick up the survivors. As the last boatload of survivors reached the stationary destroyer's side, the submarine surfaced. In trying to ram the sub which was as big as the destroyer, the destroyer itself was badly damaged, but by positioning the passengers on the starboard side, they managed to remain afloat until they were towed to safety in the Maldives. A second destroyer, however, successfully attacked the resurfacing submarine and Mrs Wright relates how satisfied they were to see it finally blown up.

Joe Eaves 'the Milk' and his wife and children in 1946. From left to right, back row: sons Ray, Trevor, Cyril, Syd and Ron. Front row: daughters Thelma and Joan, Gertrude (Joe's wife), Joe himself, daughters Glenys and Iris. The little girl in the front row is his daughter Joyce. They lived at 43 Albert Street, Pentre, and this photograph appeared in the *Rhondda Leader* in 1946, when eight members of the family were involved in the war effort. The five brothers were in the Army, Glenys and Iris were in the Land Army, and Joe was in the Special Constabulary.

Cyril Lloyd and Trevor Poole of Gelligaled in their RAF uniforms, 1944. It seems that they were both slightly worse for wear after frequenting a Treorchy public house.

Two

Working Life

Tom Giovannone from King Street, Gelli, seen here in around 1946. He is working in Fulgoni's shop in Porthcawl, in his role as manager. There is an interesting display of goods in the background.

Sheep shearing on Maindy Farm, Ton-Pentre, in 1936. The bald gentleman in middle is Mr Thomas Evans, who initially worked for Evans the brewers in Pentre. He later went to work in the colliery to earn more money.

Outside Hutching's butchers shop in October 1945. Hutching's was situated next door to Mr Francesco Giovannone's shop. The men in the photograph were most of the butcher's employees. The shop is now part of the Spar store.

Outside Francesco Giovannone's shop in Ton-Pentre in 1945. This is also now part of the Spar store. The men seen here are Francesco Giovannone and an American GI.

Outside Francesco Giovannone's shop, again in 1945. In the photograph are Rose Oliver from Gelli Road and her son Clive, as well as her niece, Margo Giovannone, whose grandfather was the shop owner.

Fred and Rose Coppolo, well-known residents of Ystrad, between 1946 and 1950. Fred and Rose owned a confectionery shop next door to Boots the chemist in Ystrad. They were renowned for their home-made ice cream, which was made from a secret family recipe.

Mrs Doris Davies of Cwmparc meets Max Boyce during a visit to the EMI factory, c. 1974. The factory which has now closed was situated between Pentre and Treorchy.

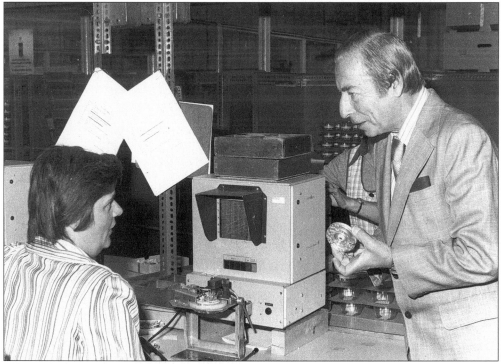

Margaret Davies of Maindy Road, Ton-Pentre, with the band leader Joe Loss on his visit to the EMI factory in 1977. Margaret was later known as Margaret Taxis, because of her now disbanded Maple Leaf Taxis (named after the emblem of Canada, her birthplace). She won many admirers for the reputation of providing a good, caring service.

One of Peglar's stores, *c.* 1940. Peglar's was a well-known chain of shops situated within the confines of the Rhondda. This particular store is believed to have been in Gelli.

Sport played an important part in working life. These are the winners of the 1928/29 Glamorgan police tug-o'-war competition were the 'G' Division, from Ton-Pentre.'

Roy Paul receives the FA Cup from the Queen on behalf of Manchester City after their 3-1 defeat of Birmingham City in the 1956 Cup Final. Roy came originally from Smith Street, Gelli.

A hazardous profession for a canary to be in! This canary was taken down the mine to test the air after the Senghenydd pit disaster.

David Davies and his brother William Davies (back row, second and third from left) originally came from Lampeter on the border of Cardiganshire and Monmouthshire. Their former home in Lampeter had been a farm where their father had married three times, each marriage producing a number of children. At the time it was customary for property to be divided between all the sons, so there was little hope of any material gain at home with such a large family. Hence, William and David, with their sisters Ellen and Maggie, moved to the Rhondda to look for work. Maggie went into service in Cardiff and Ellen stayed in the valley with her brothers to look after them. The two brothers were poor but bright and they soon found work and settled in lodgings in Tyntyla Road in Llwynypia. Frustration soon set in as they both craved an education. As they were so poor, the brothers tossed a coin to see which of them would work to help pay for the other to be educated. David lost the toss and set to work building up his own carpentry business; he never went to the mines because of poor health. William became very successful in the church, with a large parish in Bootle. He wrote books in Welsh and was also a missionary. William died of throat cancer and was given a grand funeral to which over 100 wreaths were sent. David declared that he should only have one wreath at his funeral as it had sickened him to see such wastage of money in the poor Liverpool area. This showed how much more aware David was of the poverty around him in the Rhondda. Even though David lost the coin toss, his own carpentry business became successful and he built his own house, 88 Tyntyla Road, seventy yards from where he had had his lodgings. A smart plate was erected on the front railings with his name, D.J. Davies, Builder and Undertaker, in four-inch lettering. He was very keen on education, as he had lost out himself; had he lived he would have been proud to know that all seven of his grand-children obtained degrees.

Number 88 Tyntyla Road, Llwynypia,
c. 1910. David Davies's first wife Rachel
Ann Jenkins can be seen holding one of
their children. With her is Ethel, their maid,
who later went to work in Cardiff, where
wages were better.

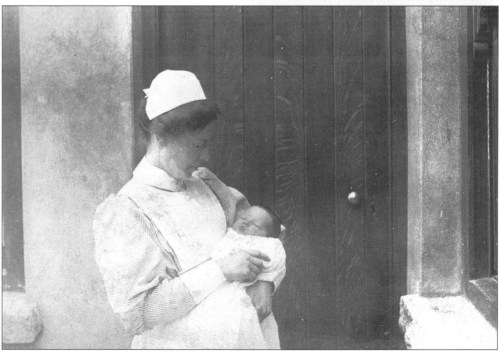

Rachel Ann Jenkins qualified as a midwife and is pictured here with a baby she has just delivered. Tragically she was herself to die in childbirth.

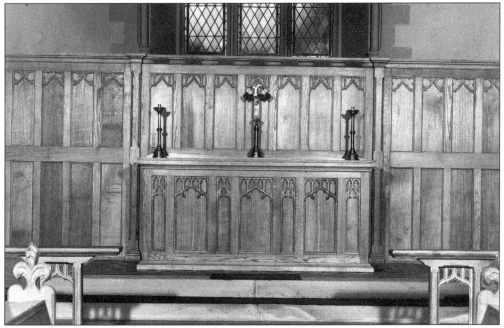

David Davies was no ordinary businessman as he was too much of a gentleman. The altar which he built in St Stephen's church, Ystrad, is just one example of this. Although he sent them a bill, in the end he never charged them a penny for the work. After his death, in 1959, his business was taken over by a Mr Stanley Morgan.

Mair Davies, pictured here in the 1940s, was one of David and Rachel's daughters. Mair followed her mother into the nursing profession.

Telephone : PENTRE 3161

5 TRAFALGAR TERRACE,
YSTRAD-RHONDDA

12 November 1959

Mrs. Davies, 88. Tyntyla Road Llwynypia

DR. TO

STANLEY MORGAN
(Late D. J. Davies and Morgan)
BUILDER AND UNDERTAKER

	£	s	d
To works of repair & alteration at 88. Tyntyla Road, Llwynypia:-			
To Labour:-			
89 Hrs @ 7/9d	34	9	9
45½ Hrs @ 7/6d	17	1	3
To materials:-			
Casement Windows Glazed & Primed and fitted with fasteners 5ft 9" x 3ft 4"	11	10	0
6ft 9" Skirting @ 2/- per ft. 12/-: 4ft 6 - 6 x 1 @ 10d 3/10	14	10	
2 pairs 2" Butt Hinges @ 2/6		5	0
2 casement fasteners 5/-: 2 basement Stays 5/-		10	0
3 ft 5"x3" @ 2/1 6/3: 3 ft door Sill @ 2/- 4/6d	6	10½	
½ Ton Sand 20/-: 2½ cwt cement @ 8/9d	1	1	10
30 Bricks @ 3d: 4/6		7	6
11 yards 6x6" White Tiles @ 21/6 per yd	11	16	6
36 Black Edge Tiles @ 10d 30/-: 5.6 lbs plaster 9/-	1	19	0
2½ Gallons Richardson @ 35/- per Gallon	4	17	6
6ft 2½" Downpipe @ 19/- ½ cwt Cement 5/0	1	14	0
Haulage		15	0
£	87	2	0

This bill, dated 12 November 1959, is for work done on David Davies' house, 88 Tyntyla Road. It is interesting to compare the costs with today's building prices.

William John Rees, of Cwmparc, late 1920s. He is shown here in his St John Ambulance Brigade uniform, of which he was a member of the Pentre Section. Mr Rees was also a haulier at the Dare Colliery. Sadly, he died prematurely from injuries he received while working at the pit. He was kicked in the chest by a horse.

Tynewbedw and Pentre Ambulance Division, 1911.

A typical example of a haulier working above one of the valley pits, *c*. 1905.

COAL MINING- TUGGING FROM SPOUT HOLE.

This photograph of a child mining coal, around 1900, shows one of the more unhealthy aspects of Rhondda's mining history. Child employment in the mines first occurred in the first half of the nineteenth century, when boys as young as six or seven were employed, mainly as door boys. Door boys opened doors for the coal drams and for ventilation purposes, preventing a build up of gases. Their life was hard, working in total darkness and alone, usually for twelve hours at a time. It was, however, an important job and it seems absurd that the whole safety of the mines could depend on these young children. Other boys worked as hauliers, filled trams or were put in charge of pumps. As a result, their schooling, if any, was infrequent and their health suffered. A report in 1842 commented that, although the children at first would become peculiarly well-developed and muscular, their unnatural strength soon diminished and they became pallid, underdeveloped, crippled and subject to chronic chest complaints, which were very often fatal. Many children were killed in pit disasters as they worked alongside men. By 1842, with the passing of the Mines Regulation Act, employment of boys underground was restricted to boys of ten and over. However, this law was usually flouted as a man could earn more for his family when he had a 'helper'. The boys were often hidden by their fathers to avoid detection whenever the mines were inspected.

A wonderful example of a miner's attire at the turn of the century. The picture was taken at one of the Rhondda pits but the exact location is unknown.

The interior of a drinking house in the early twentieth century. This particular establishment is believed to have been in Treorchy.

At the far right is the late Gladys Poole (*née* Morgan) of Gelligaled Road, Ystrad, in her first job at a draper's store in Porth in the early 1920s.

John's corner shop, Bailey Street, Ton-Pentre, in 1999. Traditional corner shops are fast disappearing and this is one of the few remaining. There was a time when every other street had its own corner shop, but as years pass and owners either move on or pass away, the shops were boarded up and converted back into houses.

Three

In the Locality

Lower Ystrad, *c.* 1950. This is now the site of Ystrad railway station and a nursing home occupies the ground on the other side of the tracks.

An aerial photograph of Ystrad through to Treorchy, 1962/3. This picture was taken by a Russian spy satellite.

Ystrad Rhondda, showing Gelligaled recreation ground, *c.* 1950. The open-air baths can be seen next to the river.

View of Ystrad showing Bodringallt School, *c.* 1950.

Gelligaled, Ystrad, *c.* 1905. This picture was taken before the road was built to Penrhys. The Gellidawel Hotel on the immediate right was demolished in 1913.

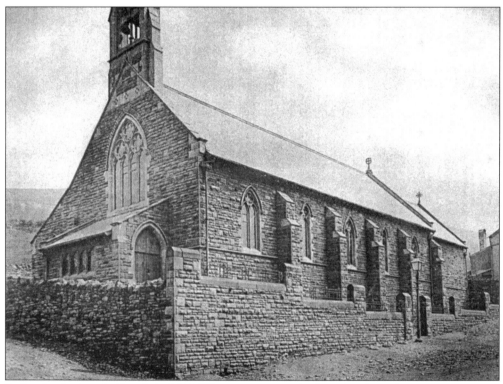

St Stephen's church, Ystrad, in 1910. This area is now a built-up residential one.

Llwynypia Hospital and the homes nearby, around 1925. Llwynypia farmhouse can be seen on the mountain top.

A view of early construction of Ystrad Sports Centre, probably in 1973. The centre was completed and opened in 1975.

Gelligaled Road, *c*. 1935. Note the Star Hotel, built on the site of the Gellidawel Hotel, which was demolished in 1913. Tramlines are visible in the road.

Gelligaled Road, Ystrad, *c*. 1900. Ystrad Conservative Club is to the right of the picture.

A view of William Street, Ystrad, *c.* 1895.

Bethel chapel, Ystrad, in 1910. This is now the site of Ystrad Boys' Club.

Ystrad Road and Free Library, Ystrad, around 1910. The library was situated near to where the new Gelli Junior School has recently been built.

Lower Gelli and Ystrad Rhondda in the early 1940s.

42

Tyisaf Road, Gelli, *c.* 1905. This is popularly known to the local community as being the approach to Carter's Corner.

Rees Street, Gelli, during the floods of December 1960. The floods caused chaos and hardship for the residents of the area over a number of days.

Smith Street, Gelli, 3 December 1960. The only way to get home that day was in a rowing boat.

Another view of the floods of December 1960, this time looking down the steps that lead from Gelli Road. This scene must evoke a lot of painful memories for the people of Gelli.

Rees Street, Gelli, 1960s. 'Don't worry love, there'll be another boat along in five minutes.'

A repeat of the flooding occurred in 1970, again in Gelli. The repeated devastation and dislocation caused by the water prompted an outcry from the residents to the authorities, who were exhorted to try and resolve the area's drainage problems.

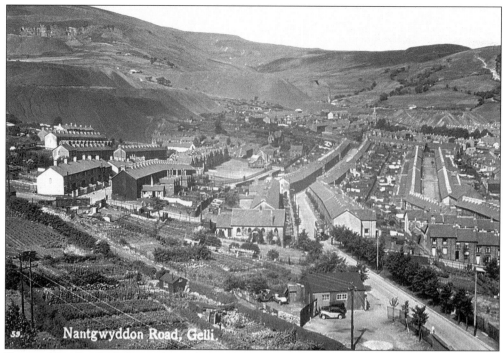

Nantgwddon Road, Gelli, in the mid-1930s. The garage in the foreground, right, with the car beside it is now the site of Richie's garage.

Gelli, Ton-Pentre and Upper Rhondda, *c.* 1975. In the background, centre, can be seen Gelli Park and Ton-Pentre football pitch.

A general view of Ton-Pentre in 1940. In the foreground can be seen the Bridgend Hotel, now demolished.

Church Road, Ton-Pentre, c. 1925. The building immediately to the left is now Hacker's the newsagents, which was a post office at the time of this photograph.

Church Street, Ton-Pentre, 1908. On the right is the Jerusalem chapel, now recently demolished.

Church Road, Ton-Pentre, in 1900, with the Workmen's Institute, now the Phoenix cinema, on the right and the Co-op on the left. The latter has since been demolished and been replaced by residential flats.

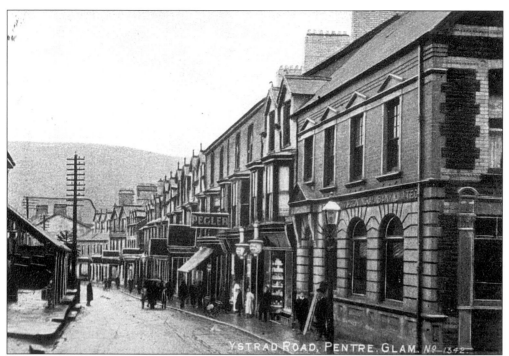

Looking down Ystrad Road, Pentre, around the turn of the century. The London and Provincial Bank on the right is now Barclays Bank.

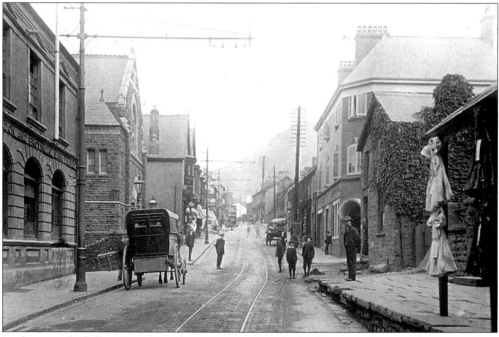

Looking up the hill in Ystrad Road, Pentre, c. 1912. The buildings on the immediate right have now been demolished. The large building on the right was then the Woodfield Public Hotel.

Llewelyn Street, Pentre, in around 1910.

Llewelyn Street, Pentre, at the turn of the century. To the immediate left are the council offices.

Llewelyn Street, Pentre, in 1970. This is a view from higher up Pentre's main road, showing the Queen's Hotel immediately to the right.

Another view of Llewelyn Street, Pentre, at the beginning of the twentieth century. Directly behind the photographer is the site of St Peter's church.

Partridge Road, Llwynypia, in the 1930s. Immediately to the right is the bus shelter that was demolished to make way for the post office which now stands in its place.

A strike march passing through Gelligaled Road, Ystrad, in 1921.

Victoria Street, Ystrad, around 1915, with Lamb Woods and the mountain behind.

St David's church, Ton-Pentre, *c.* 1900. This is now the site of Ty-Ddewi residential flats. Residents will notice that missing from the picture is Kennard Street, which was built at a later date behind the church.

Maindy Crescent, Ton-Pentre, in 1925. This road leads to 'The Maindy' giving secondary road access to Treorchy. It was built after the landslide in Pentre, which caused severe problems for those trying to travel to Treorchy.

Ton-Pentre parish church in 1904. This church was demolished to be replaced by St John's Baptist church, which opened its doors in 1987.

Dinam Park Bowling Green, Ton-Pentre, in the late 1930s. The green is now the site of a large development of Barratt houses, which were built in the early 1990s.

A general view of Ton-Pentre and Pentre in around 1965. The picture was taken from the mountain overlooking 'The Maindy'.

An early view of Pentre from the turn of the century.

Pentre Colliery, c. 1905. This gives a good view of the coal carts, indicating the high level of production at the colliery at that time.

This colliery tip slip at Pentre in 1916 caused severe access problems through the town.

Pentwyn hospital in the late 1950s. The building was situated on 'The Maindy' with a view of Pentre behind.

Pentre House and Pentre Cottage, c. 1901. This is now the site of a residential home for senior citizens, situated behind St Peter's church.

Pentre in 1908, showing the colliery in the background.

Pentre Colliery in 1900.

Ty Gwyn House, Tyntyla Road, Llwynypia, in 1912. Houses were later built, filling the gap next door. Another row of houses was added in front of the row in Tyntyla Avenue, which can be seen in the background of the picture.

Partridge Avenue, Llwynypia, in the mid-1950s. The picture, taken with an old box camera, shows some old 'prefab' houses, with Glyncornel House in the background. At the time the latter was a maternity hospital.

Another view of post-war prefab houses in the 1950s. Even to this day, in certain locations around the Rhondda valley, some of these 'temporary homes' can still be found.

Four

Schools

Bodringallt Upper School during a snowfall in the early 1980s.

Bronllwyn School in 1913. In the first half of the nineteenth century, the incidence of illiteracy was incredibly high among the working classes. The educational facilities were inadequate and learning ceased once boys reached the age at which they could go down the mines (usually six or seven) and supplement the meagre family income. For the girls, education was not considered to be that important. As long as they had learnt enough skills to become good wives and mothers, they were considered to be educated enough. There was after all at that time very little future for them beyond marriage and home life. Between 1850 and 1860, there were only three day schools in the Rhondda and consequently most working-class children depended entirely upon Sunday schools for their education. Through a succession of religious revivals in the 1850s, chapels had sprung up all over the Rhondda. These revivals were expressed through congregational singing which owed much to the combined efforts of two men, Eleazer Roberts and Revd John Roberts. They spread the knowledge of a new and simpler musical notation, developed by John Curwen, by which even young children were able to read music correctly and fluently. This was the 'Tonic Solfa' method. Taught with evangelical fervour, it spread like wildfire through Wales. Singing classes were formed through chapel, Sunday School and Band of Hope organization. All the children who attended Sunday school were taught 'Tonic Solfa'. The result of this education was that even very small children could read music. But with the high rise in population, a way had to be found to provide more schools for the mining villages. The only schools were colliery schools, promoted by coal owners and financially maintained by the miners themselves. In 1870, Forster's Education Act was passed, which attempted to give a little elementary education to every child and thus began a new era in education. It insisted on certain standards and the provision of money to build new schools where none had existed before.

'Blodeuyn Gobaith' (Flower of Hope) Sunday School, UATD Ystrad, Rhondda, c. 1916.

Principal representatives and supporters of Welsh scholars of Ton-Pentre, Gelli and Ystrad Rhondda, 1910-21.

A certificate of merit from 1914. The translation reads: 'The Independent Welsh Union of Sunday Schools. Divisional Union of Pontypridd and the Rhondda. Examination 31 March 1914. Class 1A. Children under 12 years. Certificate of Merit. Awarded to William J. Griffiths, member of Bodringallt Sunday School, after being successful in the above examination to the required standard. Secretary: Reverend T.D. Jones, Bodringallt'.

Bodringallt Junior School, Standard 2. The teacher on the right is Harold Lewis, who later became the headmaster of Gelli School.

A class photograph of pupils from Tonypandy Grammar School, 1931/2. The headmaster (on the far right) is Edward 'Bomber' Hughes. Also present are: Gwenny Jones, Lyn Davies, Betty Beynon, Margaret Evans, Mair Hughes, Margaret Davies, although their positions are unknown. The boy on the far left is Arthur Hazzard.

A class at Tonypandy Grammar School in 1934. Included in the photograph are: Lyn Davies, Florence Griffiths, Margaret Evans, Margaret Davies, M. Stretcher. The headmaster is once again Edward 'Bomber' Hughes.

The class of 1945 'Chairing of the Bard' at Pentre Secondary School on St David's Day in 1950.

A re-enactment of the 'Chairing of the Bard' at the 1994 reunion. The picture was taken at Ton-Pentre Football Club.

Ynyscynon nursery class at play in 1961.

Pontrhondda School, Llwynypia, 1962. The teacher is Mrs Morris and the pupils include: Linda John, Tina Evans, Norman Lawrence, Alwin Samuels, Sylvia Price, Jeffrey Harris, David Poole, Susan Evans, Tina Hathway, Clive Hopkins, Paul Saunders, Patrick Colman, Janet Bryant, Dianne Draper, Russel Beddows, Karen Kilslick, Rhiannon James, Tony Evans, David Roberts, Christine Ellis, Howard Jeffries, Gary Mathews, Lynda Baker, Shirley ?, Janet Williams.

Pentre Higher Grade School, sometime before 1960.

Bodringalt School, Ystrad, between 1913 and 1915.

Pupils from the Ysgol Gynradd Gymraeg in Bodringallt on a day trip in 1996 to the Ysgol Maestir, in the Welsh Folk Museum in St Fagans. The children dressed up in Victorian style for the photographs. The school was used from 1880 to 1916 and re-opened as part of the museum in 1984. Among those pictured are: Paul James, Luke ?, Lance Roberts, John Davies, Johanna Pye, Stephanie ?, Natalie Johnsson, Jake Morris, John Davies, Justin White, Rhodri ?, Michael Basset, Jonathon ?, Gareth Evans, Jay Evans, Janine ?, David John, Paul Powell, Adam Margery, Carl O'Sullivan, Rees Jonathon, David Evans, Geraint Tucker, Stacey Biggs, Christopher Owens. The teacher is Mrs Williams and the headmaster is Mr Williams, who has since retired.

Pentre Secondary School, 1950. Thelma Eaves is the third from the left on the front row.

Bronllwyn Infants' School, Gelli, in 1913.

The senior class of the Clydach Vale Schools boys' department, *c.* 1910.

Five
Sport and Leisure

Members of Ystrad Dyfodwg parish church, Ton-Pentre, enjoying one of their church outings in around 1930.

Maindy Conservative Club's rifle team, Ton-Pentre, 1928. The members are proudly displaying an impressive shield.

Ystrad Rhondda football team, c. 1930. Joe Morgan is the third from the left on the front row.

Ystrad Rhondda Football Club, *c.* 1930. William John Griffiths is second from the right on the front row.

Blodwen Owen of Tyntyla Avenue, Llwynypia prepared for a game of tennis in 1928. Blodwen passed away in 1933 after contracting TB.

Celebrations for the Coronation of Elizabeth II in the Market Square, Pentre, in 1953. The cottages in the background were demolished two years later. Included in the picture are: Christine Bosanko (peeping out from behind the flowers), Kay Sheppard, Marilyn and Diane Childs, Billy Edwards, Mrs Lowe, Mrs Sheppard, Betty Samuel, Lucy Stephens, Mrs Howells, Christine and Carol Howells, Margaret Fitzgerald, Mrs Fitzgerald, Gwyneth Edwards, Mrs Edwards, Gareth Edwards, Mrs Seal, Christine Seal, Phylis Jones, Martha Stacey, Mrs Green, Mrs Stevens, Mrs Davies, Sandra Parry, Barbara ?, Kenneth Mathews.

A children's Christmas party put on by Ton-Pentre police in 1948. It was held in Treherbert. Des Davies is at the bottom right.

Ystrad and Llwynypia lads, on one of Wales' legendary rugby trips in 1949/50. The picture was taken in London. Second from the right on the front row is Trevor Poole.

Mrs Taylor's party who travelled to Tewkesbury from Ystrad in 1936. Far left is Edwin Davies and sixth from the right on the front row is Sal Morris.

Valley locals on a day trip to Porthcawl in the early 1930s.

The wedding of Pat Oram to the Minister of Salem chapel, 1931 or 1932. Gwyneth Menna Davies is the young bridesmaid in the front row.

The bridesmaids who attended the wedding of Mr and Mrs Horace Burge at St Stephen's church, Ystrad, in 1950. From the right they are: Delma Burge, Edna Ashley, Mariann Davies, Barbara Yates, Menna Davies, Moira Johnson, Christina Baker.

Ieun Humphries (left), Thomas John Davies (middle) and Stan Bebb (right) outside 152 Parc Road, Cwmparc, in 1914 or 1915. It is interesting to note the fashion of the day.

The wedding of Thomas John Davies and Doris May Rees in 1937.

An annual outing for members of the congregation of Ystrad Dyfodwg chapel, Ton-Pentre, in 1932.

Members of Ystrad Dyfodwg chapel, Ton-Pentre, on a day trip to Hereford on 20 June 1931.

Margaret Jenkins, aged eight, c. 1910. She is dressed in traditional Welsh costume to celebrate St David's Day.

A local amateur dramatic production from the 1920s. The exact location is unknown.

A street party for the Coronation in 1953, this time in Rock Drive, Gelli. The boy in the gymslip second from the left on the front row is Jim Berry.

Two Rhondda children enjoy a day out at Ogmore in 1959.

A 1930s cricket club, possibly Ystrad. Willy John Griffiths is sitting on the ground at the front.

Ton-Pentre Cricket Club in 1925. The members include: D. Thomas, H. Royall, J.Flynn, E. Ruttley, C.W. Evans, J. Evans, A. Thomas, J. Bailey, J. Morgan, J. Whitelock, W. Davies, D. Rees.

Six

The Rhondda's
Dark Past

The caption on this picture reads: 'The Pentre Tragedy of 11 September 1904'. Crowds came from miles around to view the scene.

The Bridgend Hotel, Bridgend Square, Ton-Pentre, in the 1930s.

THE BRIDGEND HOTEL MURDER

The Rhondda, as with any industrialized and heavily-populated area, is no stranger to crime. The following tragedy, reported by the *Rhondda Leader* on Saturday 17 September 1904, was one of the more infamous cases, which 'caused immense excitement and cast a gloom over the whole of the valley'. At about 3.30 a.m. on 11 September 1904, the landlord of the Bridgend Hotel, Mr Emelyn Jones, was murdered by a burglar. The killer was a thirty-year-old man called Eric Lange. The report in the *Rhondda Leader* reads like a Victorian melodrama and was to grip the imagination of the valley's people for many months.

On the night of the murder, Eric Lange had been seen at the Bridgend Hotel drinking lemonade, but he had not stayed all evening. At approximately 1 a.m. on Sunday, Mr Emelyn Jones, after putting the nights takings plus £32 from Mr Henry Rees Davies (the butcher next door) into the safe, retired to his bedroom, where his wife Minnie and baby son Clifford had gone before. The bedroom was on the second floor of the Bridgend Hotel, with windows overlooking the railway and backyard. At around 3.30 a.m., Mrs Jones awoke to see 'by the flickering gaslight' a man crouched on the floor, 'peering at her through the foot of the bed.' Her screams caused the man to spring at her and strike her a violent blow to her temple with a jemmy. Emelyn Jones, on waking to his wife's screams, leapt out of bed and struggled with the burglar. Mrs Jones, stunned from the blow to her head, gripped the murderer's throat, but he proved too strong and, whipping out a knife from his pocket, stabbed Emelyn in the heart. At this time Clifford, the baby, was 'sleeping peacefully and in perfect innocence of the crime'. Emelyn gasped 'Oh, give me fresh air' and lived for only fifteen minutes more. His last words were, 'Oh Minnie, oh baby.' During the violent struggle, Mrs Jones called Jack 'the boots' who lived in the attic. She screamed, 'Jack, Jack, come down, someone is murdering us.' Jack came down with a revolver to help, but by then the murderer had escaped through the lavatory window by a ladder he had placed there earlier.

Ystrad station, Ton-Pentre, directly across the road from the murder scene, where the killer tried to make good his escape.

Miss Katie Richards, Emelyn's niece, who was a barmaid at the Bridgend Hotel, was woken by the screams and shouted at the riders of two passing wagons to call a doctor and the police. PC Rowe and Inspector Williams duly arrived on the scene and using their 'new technology' – their private telephone – were able to alert all the police stations in the area. There then followed a dramatic police search in which PC Williams and a plain-clothes policeman, PC Woods, managed to apprehend the murderer who was hiding behind a signal box, intending to follow the railway to Porth. He was taken by train from Pontypridd to Ystrad station, where Mrs Jones identified him as the killer from a line-up.

During Sunday, thousands of people from all parts of the valley visited the scene of the tragedy. A throng of people crowded onto the bridge, as from this point you could see the ladder which the murderer had placed against the window. On Monday 12 September, Eric Lange was brought before the magistrates at Ystrad police court in Maindy Road, Ton-Pentre, on a murder charge. 'In spite of the downpour of rain, hundreds of people unable to gain admission to the court waited in the streets ... in the hope of getting a glimpse of the accused.' At the inquest, which was on 13 September at Pentre police station before the coroner, Mr R.J. Rhys, the public were admitted to the court and there was also a large crowd outside.

They were impressed at the sight of Mrs Jones, who was dressed in deep mourning and wore a veil. She had a plaster on her temple, where she had been struck by the jemmy. The jury brought a verdict of 'wilful murder' and the coroner, a proud Welshman, expressed deep sympathy with the widow and relatives of the deceased. He stated that it was most gratifying to the public of the Rhondda Valley to know that, as in former instances, the murder had been committed not by one of themselves, but by a foreigner. The Welsh people were a most law-abiding people. They took drink and quarrelled sometimes, but they never cut each other's throats. It was a great comfort to realize this on such a painful occasion.

An early photograph of Ton-Pentre police station and courthouse, where Eric Lange was put on trial for murder.

In the *Rhondda Leader* of 24 September 1904, the funeral of Emelyn Jones was reported and there were 'affecting scenes' as Mr Jones was buried at Glyntaff Cemetery, Pontypridd. The cortège left Ystrad by a special train at 2.30 p.m. The body was enclosed in a coffin with massive brass fittings and the plate bore a simple inscription: 'John Emelyn Jones, Died Sept, 11th 1904, aged 37 years'. There was a huge concourse of people lining the route between the Bridgend Hotel and the station, the men reverently uncovering their heads as the body was borne on the shoulders of the bearers. The Revd R.D. Phillips of Cilfynydd remarked that the deceased had died heroically in defence of his wife and child.

The trial of Lange was reported in the *Rhondda Leader* on 3 December 1904, under the heading 'Prisoner Hysterical'. Lange apparently 'slouched' into the dock with 'lips firmly compressed'. There was a strange coincidence: Lange's wife, an Irishwoman called Annie Lorenz, had travelled on the same train as Mrs Jones on the way to court, unbeknown to either. Mrs Lange sat in court with her small son who, 'innocent of the grim tragedy, ate sweets with much relish.'

Mrs Jones was described as a tragic but brave figure and Lange 'shook like an aspen leaf' as her evidence was given. It was a sensational scene as Lange shivered and shook and emitted deep moans of terror and had to be physically restrained by the warders. During Mrs Jones' evidence, she cast her eyes just for a second on Lange and ' in that second the horror of the fateful and fearful night seemed reflected in the eyes of both, only the one [opposite] cowered down with terror, while the other [Mrs Jones] ... made a great effort to be brave.' During the evidence of Dr Thomas of Pentre, the prisoner was heard groaning 'Augh, no, augh!' a number of times and he 'shook so violently that his knuckle struck the front of the dock'. It was suggested by Lange's wife that he had become insane due to unemployment, but this explanation was soon rejected after the doctor's evidence was given.

Police Constable 632, early twentieth century. The officer's name is unknown. This is a typical uniform worn by constables at the time of the Pentre murder.

At 4.40 p.m. the jury retired and at 5.07 they returned with a verdict of 'guilty of wilful murder'. In a silence that could be felt, Judge Bray summed up. 'I have only one duty to perform. That is to pronounce the only sentence which the law allows in the case of wilful murder. I order that you be taken from this place to a lawful prison and thence to a place of execution, that you be hanged by the neck until you are dead and that your body be buried in the precincts of the prison in which you shall have been confined for your execution. May the Lord have mercy on your soul.' Solemn 'Amens' were heard from all parts of the court and the convict was removed to Cardiff Gaol, where the execution was to take place.

Lange's execution took place at Cardiff Gaol on Wednesday 21 December at 8 a.m. Mr Billington was the executioner. Prior to this, Lange had written a letter to Mrs Jones, from the gaol, begging her forgiveness so that he could die in peace. She declined to reply to the letter. Lange's demeanour since the conviction had, apparently, changed dramatically and after the failure to secure a reprieve, he 'was resigned to his fate and awaited his doom with great fortitude.' There was a touching scene when Lange's wife and three children visited him for the last time on 20 December. The young children were informed that they would not see their father again on this earth and Lange 'wept copiously when he kissed each of them for the last time.'

The press were allowed to witness the execution which was to take place in a small shed adjoining 'A' Block. The death chamber was opened by folding doors and the inside was lit by a single flickering gas jet attached to one of the whitewashed side walls. The hanging rope was suspended from a cross beam. Under the rope, was a chalk mark on the spot where the convict was to stand. It must have been a dismal scene that met the eyes of Lange, when he was led to the death chamber as the bell from a nearby church slowly tolled the hour of eight. As the minister pronounced the words, 'I know that my redeemer liveth,' the sentence of death was carried out.

The Bridgend Hotel in 1955. By this stage, fifty-one years after the murder, the memories of the grizzly events that took place here were fading into history.

The Griffin Hotel as it looks today, with Volunteer Street running alongside it to the right. The exterior of the pub has changed little since 1902. This is where Thomas Lewis drank before killing his girlfriend.

MURDER IN VOLUNTEER STREET

Two years before the Bridgend Hotel murder, on Saturday 26 December 1902, another local murder, this time a crime of passion, occurred in Volunteer Street, Pentre. Thomas Lewis of 15 Volunteer Street killed his lover, eighteen-year-old Ethel Adlam, also of Volunteer Street, by drowning her in the river behind the house, after a drinking binge at the Griffin pub. This murder, however, did not arouse the interest of the general public to the same degree as the Bridgend Hotel murder. In fact a great deal of sympathy was shown towards the accused and his father, even to the extent that a circle of their friends started a fund 'in order to alleviate the circumstances of the old man ... and to contribute towards the security of a sound defence for the unfortunate son.' The appeal was made through the columns of the *Rhondda Leader* and donations were to be forwarded to the treasurer, Mr William Comley of 8 Volunteer Street, Pentre.

Bridgend Square as it looks today. The Bridgend Hotel has long since been demolished and in recent years a public toilet has been erected on the site. Every day people travel past this spot, most unaware of its history.

Volunteer Street, Pentre, in 1999. This is the street where both murderer and victim lived and where events which led to the murder took place. The killer was later found hiding beneath chicken coops, apparently in a dreadful state after his sweetheart's body was found.

An early picture of Tyntyla Farm, where Jane Lewis was staying with her aunt and uncle and where she ultimately met her grisly death.

THE TYNTYLA FARM MURDER

An earlier local murder took place on Sunday night, 2 December 1862, in the wood below Tyntyla farmhouse. Details of this report come from Mr Owen Morgan in his *History of Pontypridd and the Rhondda Valleys* of 1903.

Mr Morgan was alive in 1862 and visited the site of the murder a few months after it happened and interviewed the people concerned. The victim was a twenty-three-year-old woman, Miss Jane Lewis, who was staying with her uncle and aunt, Mr and Mrs Williams, at Tyntyla Farm. On the night of 2 December 1862, she had been on her way to the Welsh Baptist chapel at Heolvach, when she was brutally murdered. Her throat was cut with a razor, which was usually located on the top of a grandfather clock in Tyntyla farmhouse and belonged to Mr Williams. It was first concluded that the victim had committed suicide, as she was found on examination to be pregnant. But this was quickly denounced as the severity of her injuries showed that they could not have been self-inflicted. Suspicion then fell on Jane's boyfriend, one Tom Williams, known as 'Tom of the screens', a man also known to be 'sober, industrious and respectable in all respects'. Tom was taken into custody that night by Sgt Wise, but was released after making a statement that although he and Jane had arranged to meet at the Baptist chapel on the Sunday at six o'clock, she had not turned up at the arranged time. Tom went to Tyntyla Farm to find out where Jane was, but

Tonypandy police station, *c.* 1890. With the fast growing population in the valleys, more police stations were needed. Ton-Pentre station was not built until 1902.

strangely, he stated that he had not gone by the shortest route, which was through the woods, but took the longer way up the slanting cart track. The other accused person was a Thomas Edmunds, a servant then working at Tyntyla Farm, who was also thought to be Jane's lover. He too was later arrested but released through lack of evidence.

So the murderer was never caught and Jane Lewis was buried at Ainon Baptist chapel in Tonyrefail. Tom Williams then took lodgings at Tonyrefail, within 100 yards of her grave. But he was a broken man and 'appeared on the verge of insanity'. He emigrated to Australia soon afterwards. However, this was not the end of the story, for about two years after the murder, near Ballarat in Australia, a Mr Richard Packer and his father were standing on their doorstep, when they observed a strange man walking along the road hurling stones at the houses. He stopped when he saw the men and, recognizing them as Welshmen, he asked them if they had heard of the murder of Jane Lewis of Tyntyla Farm. When they replied in the affirmative, he said 'it was I that killed her'. With that he walked on, restarting his strange behaviour, but he was never seen or heard of again. If this man was Tom Williams, and it seems likely that it was, it would appear that even after escaping to the other end of the world, he could not escape the memory of what he had done to Jane. It was to haunt him for the rest of his life and leave him a lonely and broken man.

Glamorgan mounted policemen, *c.* 1895. These would have been prominent figures during strikes and riots.

Church Road, Ton-Pentre, *c.* 1904. In the background is the bridge going over the railway track at Ystrad station, on which thousands went to stand on Monday 12 September 1904 to look at the scene of the Bridgend Hotel murder.

During the strikes in 1910/11 police officers were brought in from other divisions to deal with the riots that ensued. The above officers armed with rifles were brought in for this purpose.

These officers from the early twentieth century are believed to be from Ton-Pentre police station. It is thought that they are pictured in the backyard of the station.

This group of Caernarfon police were brought in to cover the Tonypandy coal strike in 1911. The number of officers brought in from outside gives an insight into the scale of the strike and how high the miners' emotions were running at that time.

'C' Division, Glamorganshire constabulary, on strike duty in Penygraig and Tonypandy, 1920.

C' Division, Glamorgan police in 1911. They were called in to cover the Tonypandy coal strikes.

The late Police Sergeant (PS) Baker's funeral leaving Penygraig, 27 February 1918. PS Baker tragically died at an early age after an appendix operation. This goes to show that it was not only crime that cruelly claimed lives at an early age. It was not until the late twentieth century that medical practice advanced to the standard that we expect today.

Seven
Further Afield

The statue of a miner and his wife in Llwynypia. It is a fitting tribute to those who gave their all to the mining industry.

Llwynypia Road leading to Tonypandy, *c.* 1900. The large building on the right is V.T. Parry's emigration agency. The building later became the post office, which has since closed. The fire station is now opposite this building, along with the sea scouts' centre and Llwynypia day centre.

A railway accident at Fernhill Colliery, Treherbert, in 1895.

An early motoring accident, c. 1915. Such a gathering would now never be seen in the valley, as crashes involving cars are now regular occurrences and do not prevoke much interest. Here the number of spectators viewing the carnage suggests the rarity of such incidents then and the excitement they caused.

St Albans Road and church, Blaenrhondda, *c.* 1915. Fernhill working men's hall is in the background.

Fernhill working men's hall in around 1938, with a backdrop formed by Penpych mountain. The working men's hall was demolished a few years ago to make way for sheltered accommodation.

Treherbert open-air swimming pool, which opened in 1936. It is seen here in around 1950. The pool remains in use to this day, although it has now been converted to an indoor pool.

Treorchy cricket ground in the early 1920s. The pavilion was built in mock Tudor style and is still the scene of many sporting events.

Wesleyan Central Hall, Tonypandy, nearing completion in 1923. It was built on the site of a smaller chapel. The late Viscount Lord Tonypandy began his oratorical career here. The building later became known as the Methodist Central Hall. It was demolished in the mid-1970s and the shopping complex where Somerfields and Peacocks are situated was constructed in its place in the mid-1980s.

Treorchy Scouts in the 1920s. The Scouts were popular in the valley at this time. Even to this day the Beavers, Cubs and Scouts are popular, with a local Beavers club running in Pentre.

Treorchy railway station, with the last working steam train to run through the valley, on her way to Treherbert.

The first tram trip in the Rhondda – the 'Ferndale Tram' – in 1908.

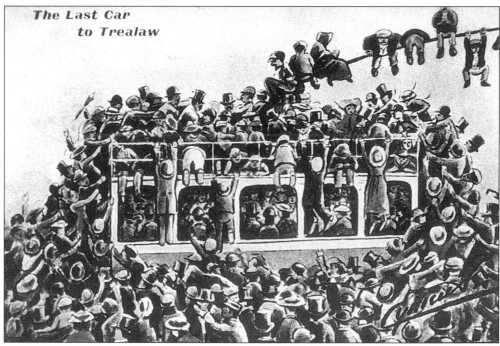

A cartoon depiction of the last tram to Trealaw. The last tram was withdrawn from service on 1 February 1934, when technology progressed and motorized buses began their service to the public.

Prospect Place, Edwardsville, near Treharris in Merthyr Tydfil. On 27 October 1913 a tornado tore through Edwardsville; the devastation caused to Prospect Place by this rare event is clearly seen here.

Cardiff Arms Park in the 1960s. The Arms Park has for a long time been a Mecca for the Rhondda rugby fans on their annual 'Rugby trips'. However, this historic ground has now been demolished to be replaced by a new domed ground, the Millenium Stadium.

105

Western Town, Blaenrhondda, under construction in the mid-1980s. The town, although a bold planning idea, was poorly attended and was destined to failure within a short space of time.

Dan Jones' Central Auction Mart in Porth, *c.* 1925. As an auctioneer and fruit merchant he struggled to make a living, as so many others did during this era. Note the box of 'ripe' bananas on the cart.

The photograph below shows the cremation in Caerlan Fields on top of the hill of Dr William Price in 1893. Dr William Price of Llantrisant was a strange and remarkable man, who held strong beliefs. He scorned orthodox religion for its hypocrisy and puritanical ways. He hated the law and frequently fought against it and, although a doctor and surgeon himself, he mistrusted contemporary medical theories and practice. He was an advocate of free love, championed the cause of unmarried mothers and, although himself the father of several children, he never married. However he lived intimately with Gwenllian Llewelyn, the mother of two of his children, until his death in 1893. Dr Price, born on 4 March 1800, will be remembered primarily as the pioneer of Welsh cremation. One of his beliefs was that burial in the ground was unhygienic, unscientific and unpleasant and that it results in wastage of good land, pollution of the earth, water and air, and is a constant danger to all living creatures. As a result of this, when his beloved five-month-old son, Iesu Grist, died on 10 January 1884, he took the body to the summit of the hill on Caerlan Fields and proceeded to cremate it. As locals left their chapels on this Sunday night and saw this strange (and to them blasphemous) spectacle on the mountain, there was uproar and an angry mob gathered. Police were called and they retrieved the half-burned body of the child from the flames and arrested Dr Price as a heretic. In the ensuing trial, Dr Price was vindicated and on 21 March succeeded in finishing the cremation of his son. During the trial, Dr Price received thousands of letters from people commending his courage, but local opinion remained strongly against his unchristian ways. In the years following, he would occasionally cremate his dead cattle to prove his beliefs and probably also out of sheer devilry. These events still caused a stir in the neighbourhood, but ultimately helped to champion his cause.

When he died on Tuesday 23 January 1893, his last words were 'Give me champagne', which was what he always drank when he felt unwell. His last wish was to be cremated on Caerlan Field at a spot he had marked some months earlier with a 60ft pole, surmounted by a crescent-shaped representation of a new moon. He desired that there should be no sorrowing and that no mourning clothes should be worn. The cremation took place on 31 January 1893 before thousands of people who had travelled to Llantrisant town. The service was conducted by Revd Daniel Fisher and was read in Welsh, but the phrase 'consigned to the earth' had been changed to 'consigned to the fire'. Dr Price's ashes were scattered to the four winds, to 'help the grass grow and the flowers to bloom'. Thus died a Welsh legend, a naturalist, a druid and pioneer of Welsh cremation.

The cremation of William Price in Caerlan Field in 1893, seen from Llantrisant Town.

THE SENGHENYDD TRAGEDY

The next four pages show in graphic detail the events surrounding the Senghenydd pit disaster of Tuesday 14 October 1913, in which 440 men died after an explosion in the Universal Colliery at Senghenydd. The Universal had already claimed the lives of eighty-one miners in explosion on 24 May 1901, but due to the inability to learn from the mistakes made then, along with the sheer negligence of the pit owners, the tragedy of 1913 was to become the worst disaster in British mining history. The story is included here as a tribute and a reminder of all the similar tragedies that occurred throughout the South Wales mining communities. In an industry that was no stranger too disaster, danger and death, the true cost of coal is shown only too clearly.

It is very easy, as we approach a new millennium, to look back at the mining disasters of South Wales and not see beyond the facts and figures given. Behind each death there is a family left behind and in Senghenydd, nearly every house and family was affected by the tragedy. Mining disasters are also unique in that they discriminate. They pick out the male members of a community and also only those of the lower class. The Senghenydd community lost a large percentage of its menfolk and therefore also its breadwinners, for in a single-industry community there was little other employment. Out of the 440 who died that day, twenty-three were aged between fourteen and sixteen. Ironically, the next year saw the outbreak of the First World War, which further drained the community of its men. In the seventeen years from the 1901 pit disaster to the end of the war, the community lost 600 of its menfolk. These pictures, then, help us to go beyond the facts and figures. They portray the real suffering, the stark reality of a community that, although no stranger to death, had no other option than acceptance. Senghenydd is a mirror to all the other mining disasters that occurred in South Wales. These pictures reflect the scenes and faces of Senghenydd on the tragic morning of 14 October 1913, but they could be scenes that accompanied any other mining disaster in South Wales. It was an industry united in danger and death, where men, in order to earn the little that they did, were willing to pay with their lives.

A group of children wait for news of relatives after the explosion at the pit.

The true reality of the coal industry: some of the 447 bodies are removed from the pit.

Hour by hour, one by one, all through the day as many of the 440 victims as possible were recovered and brought to the surface. However it was about two months before the final victim was recovered.

The scene outside the mortuary at Senghenydd. How thankful we should be that improvements since 1913 enables us to avoid tragedies of this type and scale again.

These corrugated-iron and tar-painted huts were built to house the shaft sinkers and railway construction workers for the Universal at Senghenydd. Six of the residents living in these huts perished in the 1913 explosion.

One of the many funeral processions that passed through Senghenydd, marking the grief and pain that united a community.

Fernhill Colliery at Blaenrhondda, Treherbert, around 1910. This scene is a typical example of the dismal and dangerous conditions that were experienced by so many men.

Judges Hall soup kitchen in Tonypandy, 1926. Edwin J. Davies is second from the left in the front row.

Central Hall, Tonypandy, in its heyday in the 1930s. Many a happy hour was spent here. It is now the site of Somerfields.

Miskin Road, Trealaw, opposite the site of Leekes, in the mid-1950s. The garage in the foreground is now a small general store.

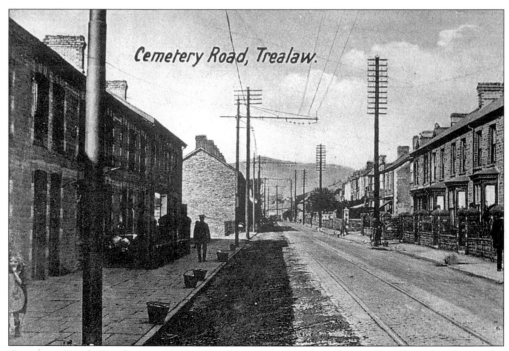

Cemetery Road, Trealaw, *c.* 1920. The phrase 'putting the ashes out', still used today in the valley, originated from the practice of leaving the buckets of ashes on the pavement for disposal by the 'ash man'.

Ynysbwl Co-operative Society Ltd, c. 1910. This picture displays the fashions of the time and also the elaborate displays. The Co-ops were opened throughout the valley, with many miners' families having accounts in these stores. In later years, Co-op stamps were collected and used to obtain goods.

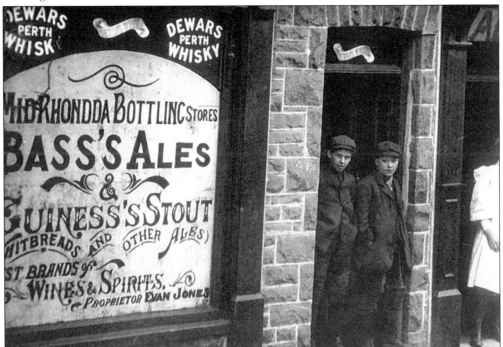

A fine example of an alehouse window in around 1912, typical of the frontage on pubs at the time. The miners who frequented the alehouses believed that a glass of ale would help to stave off the effects of dust on the chest. Ale however was probably cleaner than water to drink, as in these times many diseases – notably typhoid – were spread through poor sanitary conditions.

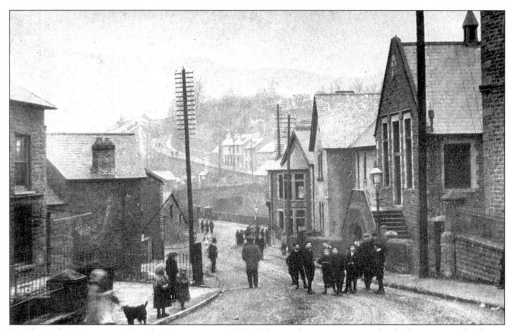

Porth police station, Porth Street, in 1905. The police station, which has recently been demolished, was in recent years widely reputed to be haunted, causing a few policemen to shiver and grimace at the thought of having to work alone in the building!

The old bridge at Porth in the 1930s. The bridge now no longer exists, but was situated near to where today's bridge stands to provide access up to Cymmer hill.

Treorchy recreation ground in the 1930s. In the background is 'The Maindy' with the Gorsedd stones in view. The stones are now surrounded by houses and the cul-de-sac is known as Druids Close. To the right of the picture the Ysbyty George Thomas (hospital) is now in place and 'The Maindy' itself is covered in trees, planted by the Forestry Commission.

The New Schools in Treorchy, c. 1910. They were built at a time when the surge in the population required more schools to be built and the focus on education became more important.

The shrine, St Mary's Well, Penrhys. This was originally a place of pilgrimage, formerly housed in a wooden building. The original shrine is believed to have been burned in 1538 on the orders of Thomas Cromwell.

The statue of Our Lady of Penrhys on the top of Penrhys mountain. The statue is a place of prayer, in association with the shrine. The statue replaces the original, which was blue and gold and the object of many a pilgrim's journey.

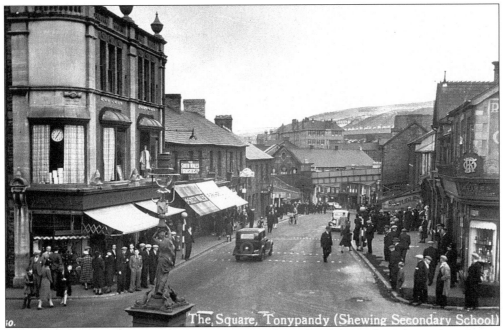

The Square, Tonypandy, in the 1930s. The secondary school shown here (centre) no longer exists; in its place is a car park where every Friday the local market is held.

Dunraven Street, Tonypandy, c. 1900. This is still a busy place today and due to the volume of shoppers and traffic, the area has recently been turned into a pedestrian precinct.

Dinas Junior Boys' School, 1933. The school team were the winners of the Mid-Rhondda Junior Championship.

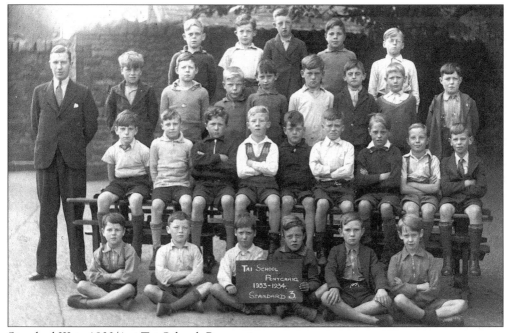

Standard III in 1933/4 at Tai School, Penygraig.

A working steam train wends its way through the valley at Blaencwm, near Treherbert, in the early 1950s.

A lone watcher enjoys the view of a steam train as it leaves Treherbert station in the early 1950s. In 1954/5 diesel trains replaced the steam trains, thus ending the era of steam in the valley.

Local valley boys on a day trip in the early twentieth century. Privately owned horse-drawn brakes provided a service between the valleys from the late 1870s until 1908, charging a flat-rate fare of a penny.

A 1920s charabanc carries Rhondda people on an outing to Gough's caves, Cheddar.

John and Elizabeth Ann Morgan with their children in 1904. Gladys is sitting on John's knee and Joe is in the background with Edith, Carrie and baby Mary Ann. The family moved to Tyntyla Avenue, Llwynypia, and were one of the first families to move into the newly built council houses that were erected in 1924.

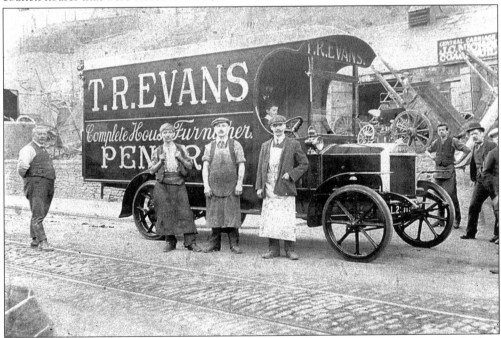

T.R. Evans, furniture manufacturer, retailer and auctioneer, *c.* 1920. The company had an impressive presence in Pentre. In the background are the premises of a coach builder.

High Street, Ferndale, in around 1900, before the trams arrived. Ferndale has changed little since those times.

The Industrial Co-operative society, Ferndale, c. 1905. The staff are all gathered for the rare chance of a photograph to be taken.

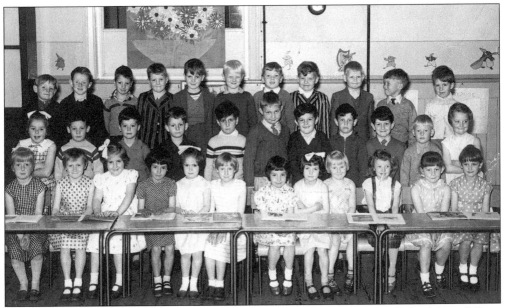

Cwmparc Juniors in 1966. From left to right, back row: Mark Philips, David Lloyd, David King, -?-, William Eveleigh, Alan Clarke, Ralph Humphries, -?-, Geraint Thomas, Danny Hamer, John Davies. Middle row: Sharon Williams, Paul Thomas, Phil Smith, Lyn Evans, Dai Thomas, Ken Latton, David ?, William Thomas, Islwyn Mundy, -?-, -?-. Front row: -?-, Denise Astley, Jane Evans, Leslie Davies, -?-, Christine Oliver, Sian Williams, Ruth Mars, Kim Trott, -?-, -?-, Andrea Jones.

Cwmparc Infants in 1962/3. From left to right, back row: Dai Lloyd, Phil Smith, Islwyn Mundy, Geraint Thomas, Dave Thomas, Lyn Evans. Second row: Stephen Evans, -?-, Sharon Williams, -?-, Ken Latton, -?-, -?-, Janice Beacham, William Evely. Front row: Ruth Mars, Mark Philips, David King, Denise Astley, Kim Trott, -?-, Sian ?, Wayne George, John Davies, Andrea Jones.

After undertaking a pictorial journey through our history, including the distant and the more recent past, what picture does the Rhondda conjure up in our minds? Some see it as being like this one: a picture of poverty, desolation and hopelessness...

...while others prefer to see this, another side of the Rhondda. This is the annual Rhondda Fun Run. We in the valley would like to believe in the more optimistic view, a living testimony to a community spirit that is still alive and well. It is a strong and vibrant spirit that will continue to form the strong base upon which future generations will stand and thrive. Those of us who may leave the Rhondda and become part of other communities in other parts of the world will never forget the place that gave them spirit and strength; always their roots will be fondly remembered when they think of their homeland, the Rhondda.

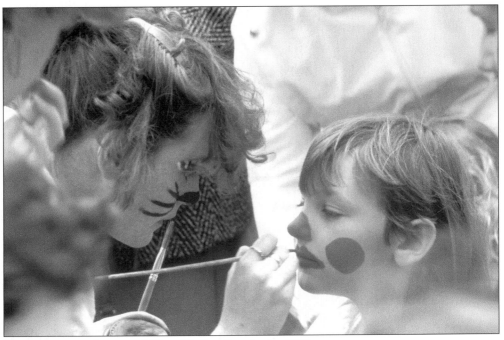
Face painting at the annual Rhondda Fun Run in the 1980s.

Fun Run spectators at Ystrad Sports Centre in the 1980s. These crowds turned out to cheer the Fun Run competitors on, support local charities and just enjoy a good day out with their families.

Welsh costume at the turn of the century. This is a wonderful example of a Welsh lady in traditional costume carrying her baby in a shawl in a manner not untypical for the day.

Acknowledgements

The authors would like to thank the following for the help that they gave us in order that this book could be compiled:

Philip Evans, Mary Lock, Tony Skates, Elma Roberts, Christine Bosanko, Joe Harris, Mr Evans, Mrs Griffiths, Jeremy Mann and the Bridgend Police Museum, Alan Jones, Al the barber, Margo Giovannone, The Governor of HM Prison Cardiff, Mrs Evans, Treorchy Library, Des Davies, and anyone else that we have failed to mention.

Thank you all.